HEROES OF LIBERTY

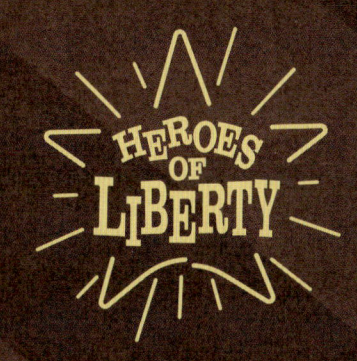

American values, one story at a time.

Sean B. Dickson

Thomas Sowell – A Self-Made Man

Illustrations by Carl Pearce

Text copyright © Heroes of Liberty Inc., 2021

Illustrations copyright Heroes of Liberty Inc., 2021

1216 Broadway, New York, NY 10001

All rights reserved. No part of this book may be reproduced or transmitted in any form or by any means, electronic or mechanical, including photocopying, recording, or by any information storage and retrieval system without written permission from the publisher.

Heroes of Liberty Inc.
1216 Broadway, New York, NY 10001

Find more heroes to read about on:
WWW.HEROESOFLIBERTY.COM

HEROES OF LIBERTY

Thomas Sowell

A SELF-MADE MAN

Thomas Sowell

spent his life studying social and economic questions. He wanted to find out how people could improve their lives and how America, the most free country in the world, enables them to do so.

He has written many books explaining what he's learned over the years. But what he has to teach us is not only in his books; his life story tells us a lot too.

Thomas Sowell started out in life at a huge disadvantage. He was raised by his great aunt in a poor town in the South. Growing up, he never got the chance to know his mother and father. And he often had no money for new shoes or even for bus fare.

But Thomas Sowell succeeded because wherever he went, and whatever he did, he never accepted anything he didn't think he deserved. He wanted nothing unearned and asked for nobody's pity.

Thomas Sowell was determined to make it on his own. And he did.

RECEIVED DOCTORATE IN ECONOMICS FROM THE UNIVERSITY OF CHICAGO — 1968
CHICAGO, ILLINOIS

BECAME SENIOR FELLOW AT THE HOOVER INSTITUTION — 1980
STANFORD, CALIFORNIA

PROFESSOR AT CORNELL
UNIVERSITY – 1965-1969
ITHACA, NEW YORK

GRADUATED FROM HARVARD
UNIVERSITY – 1958
BOSTON, MASSACHUSETTS

ENTERED STUYVESANT
HIGH SCHOOL – 1945
NEW YORK CITY, NEW YORK

BORN
JUNE 30, 1930
GASTONIA,
NORTH CAROLINA

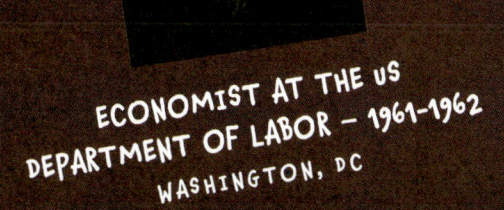

ECONOMIST AT THE US
DEPARTMENT OF LABOR – 1961-1962
WASHINGTON, DC

Thomas Sowell was born in 1930, in Gastonia, North Carolina, during the time of segregation in the South. Back then, many Americans lived in conditions that are hard for us to imagine today. There were homes without running hot water, electricity, or indoor toilets.

Thomas's childhood home was like this. The Sowells had to use kerosene lamps for light, and when Tommy—as he was called when he was little—needed a bath, they would heat the water on a woodburning stove and fill up a portable tin tub.

But Tommy didn't know he was poor. He just thought this was how everyone lived. He didn't know any rich people, so he had nothing to compare his experience to.

The woman who raised Tommy was named Molly. She was his father's aunt. But Tommy just called her Mama.

Tommy never met his father because he passed away before Tommy's mother, Willie, gave birth to him. When Tommy's father learned he was sick, he asked his aunt to take in Tommy and raise him as her own. This is because Willie already had four children, you see, and the money she earned as a maid wasn't enough to support another child.

When Tommy was still small, Willie would sometimes come over to visit. She just had to see her little boy, even if only for a little while. Neither Willie nor Aunt Molly told Tommy who she really was, though.

Willie always took it hard. She would bite her lip to keep from crying, and her heart would break each time she left.

But Tommy was not a sad boy—not at all. Aunt Molly had two grown daughters, Birdie and Ruth, and they loved Tommy very much. Birdie, especially, was very close with Tommy, and she pampered him whenever she could.

The Sowells didn't have many books. There were a few illustrated ones for children, and they had the Bible, of course. But these were enough for Birdie to teach Tommy to read. By age four, he could read on his own.

Aunt Molly also had a partner whom Tommy called Daddy. He was very active in his church. He was also very proud to be a light in Baby Tommy's life. He took little Tommy to church, and—with a baby bottle in his pocket—made an announcement to the congregation.

"Folks," he said, "I no longer have time for my church duties. Now I have a beautiful baby boy who depends on me."

When Tommy grew up, he used to love to hear this story, although of course, he was too young to remember it himself.

Back then, in the town of Gastonia, South Carolina, nearly everyone in Tommy's neighborhood was black. These were the days of Jim Crow laws in the South. These laws separated Americans based on color. It was unfair. Blacks had to go to separate schools, ride separately in buses, and eat at separate restaurants. So when Tommy was little, he rarely saw white people at all. In fact, when he did see white people, they were usually characters in comic books.

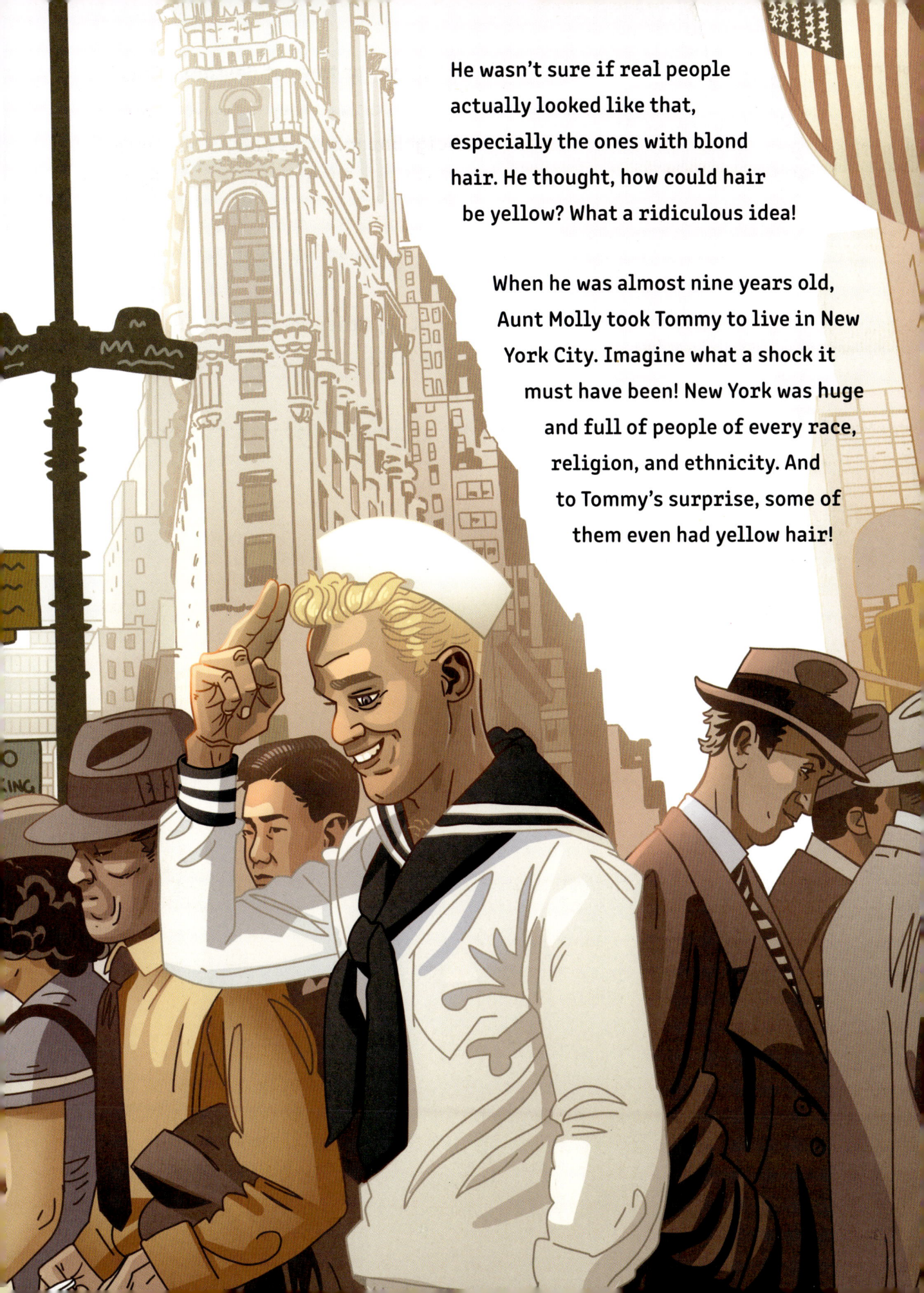

He wasn't sure if real people actually looked like that, especially the ones with blond hair. He thought, how could hair be yellow? What a ridiculous idea!

When he was almost nine years old, Aunt Molly took Tommy to live in New York City. Imagine what a shock it must have been! New York was huge and full of people of every race, religion, and ethnicity. And to Tommy's surprise, some of them even had yellow hair!

The teachers in New York thought an education down South wasn't worth very much. So when Tommy first arrived at his new school, they figured he'd be better off repeating third grade.

Tommy didn't like that. He didn't like that at all. "I'm not going to third grade," he informed the teachers. "I'm going to fourth."

"It's not up to you, child," said a tall teacher with a long face.

"Then I'd like to see the principal," Tommy replied.

The teachers were puzzled. Aren't children supposed to be afraid to see the principal?

"He's too busy now," said a teacher with a red tie, folding his arms on his chest.

"Well, I'll wait, then," said Tommy. He folded his arms on his chest too. The teachers looked at each other. Maybe the principal could teach this kid a lesson, they thought.

But the principal was amused—and a little curious too. Who is this headstrong nine-year-old, he wondered, and how on earth did he become so self-confident?

63 + 776 =
164 + 39 =
473 + 317 =
492 + 296 =

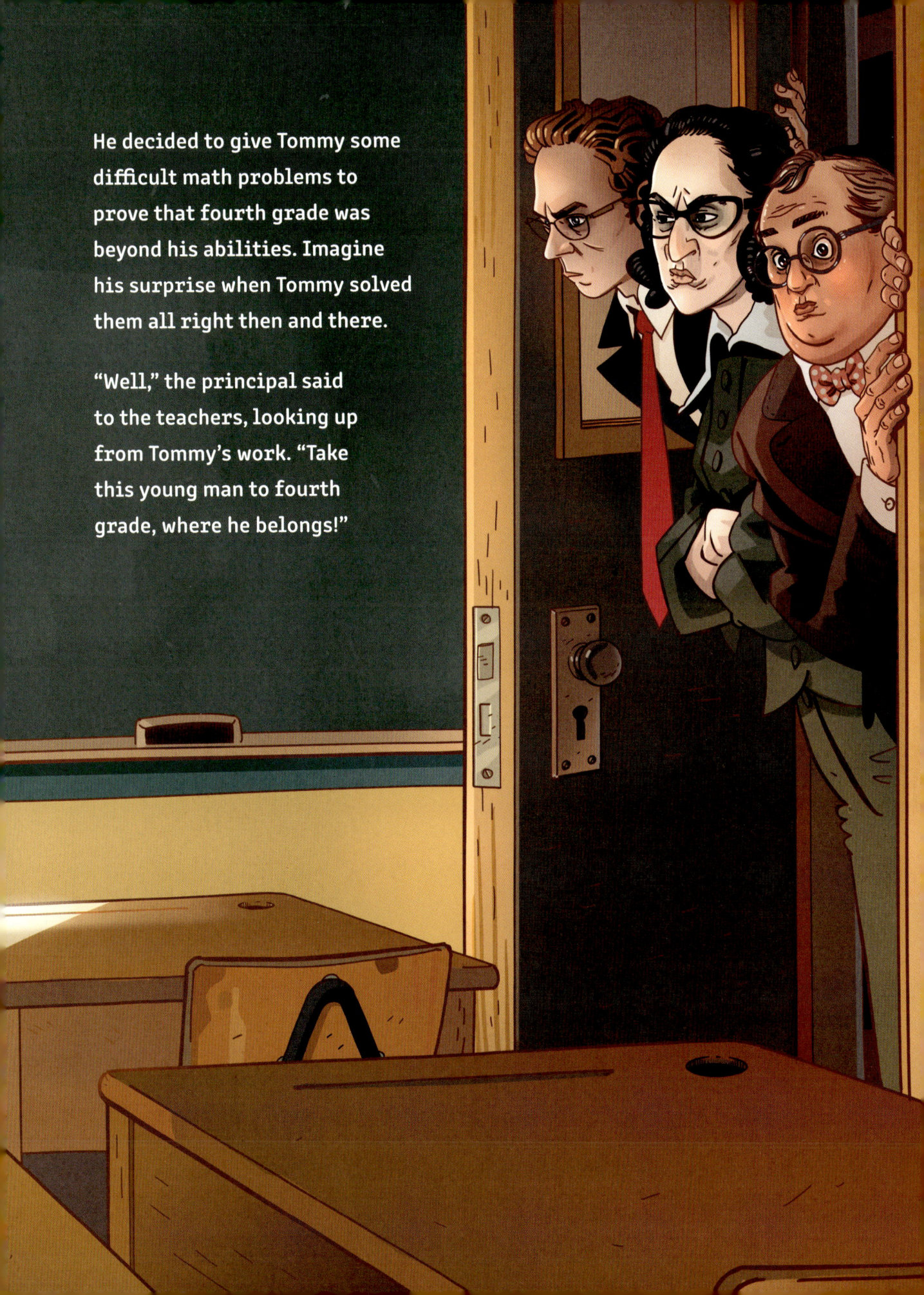

He decided to give Tommy some difficult math problems to prove that fourth grade was beyond his abilities. Imagine his surprise when Tommy solved them all right then and there.

"Well," the principal said to the teachers, looking up from Tommy's work. "Take this young man to fourth grade, where he belongs!"

Tommy loved baseball and could hold his own there too. He wasn't the best player, but he wasn't the worst one either. And above all, he really liked to play. So, he didn't appreciate it when, one day, a bunch of older boys tried to take over the field in the middle of a game.

"Don't mind them," Tommy said to his friends. "Just keep playing."

When one of the older boys—one much bigger and taller than Tommy—told him to beat it, Tommy looked him right in the eye. "You'll have to make me do that," he said. Then he tightened his grip on the bat. He was going to stand his ground, come what may.

The older boy glanced back at his friends, then down at Tommy, and then at the bat. "Well...whatever," he muttered. Then he turned and walked away.

Yes, Tommy was a very stubborn kid. Which was sometimes a good thing—and sometimes, well, not so much.

Tommy's grades were very good. So, he was accepted to one of New York's best schools: Stuyvesant High School. It was a very demanding place. There was so much homework that Tommy often had to stay up late at night to do it all. Sometimes he finished only after sunrise, just in time to get ready for school.

And when the weekend came around, Tommy still had no time to relax. His family couldn't afford his subway rides to and from school, or the food for his lunch.

So, he had to pay for it all himself. He spent the weekends running up and down the Sugar Hill neighborhood of Harlem delivering groceries.

Because Tommy was the first member of his family to go to high school, Aunt Molly couldn't understand why he had to spend so much time in the library. Why couldn't he work in the afternoons to help the family out? They began to argue. She would shout at him and he would shout right back.

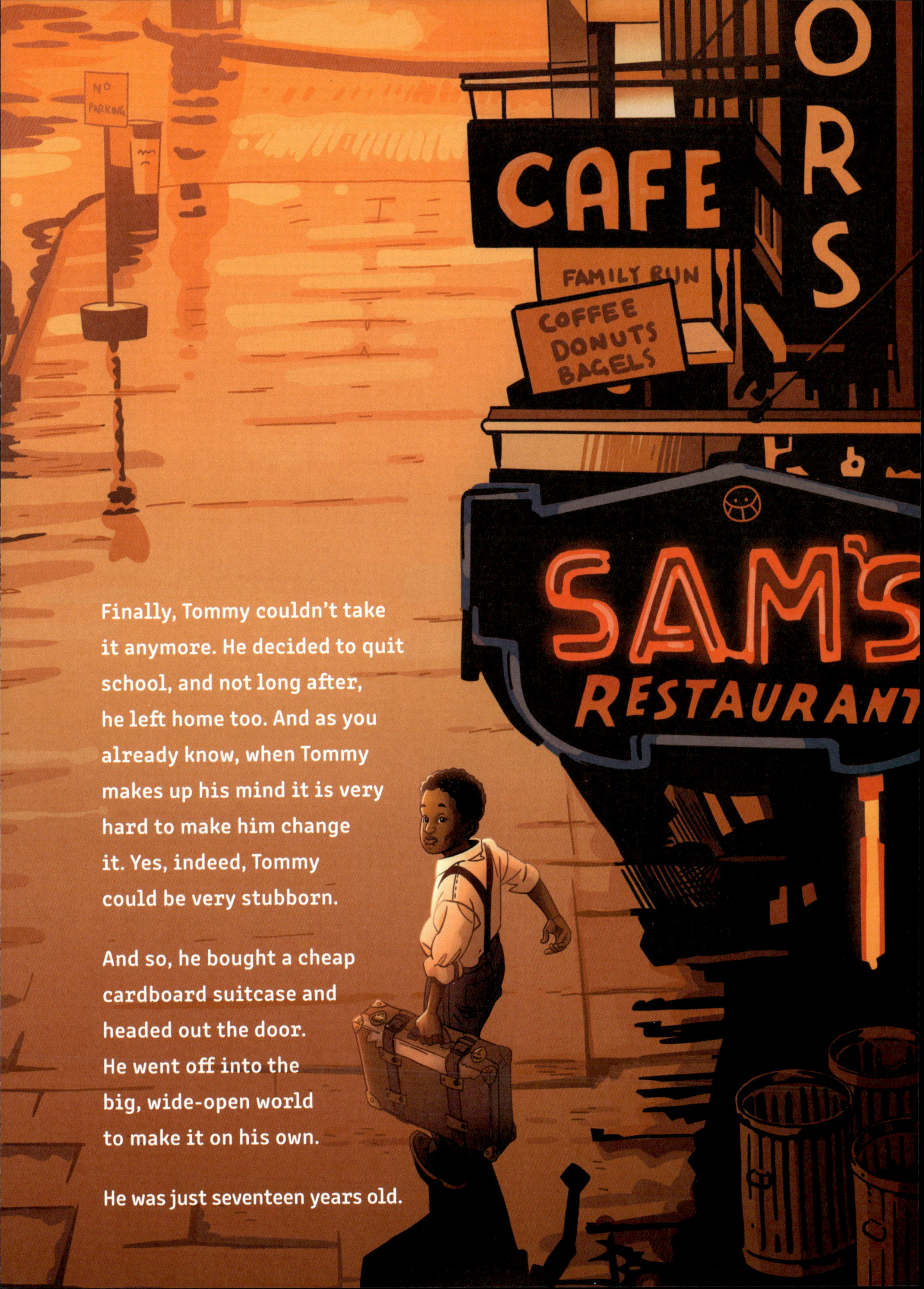

Finally, Tommy couldn't take it anymore. He decided to quit school, and not long after, he left home too. And as you already know, when Tommy makes up his mind it is very hard to make him change it. Yes, indeed, Tommy could be very stubborn.

And so, he bought a cheap cardboard suitcase and headed out the door. He went off into the big, wide-open world to make it on his own.

He was just seventeen years old.

For the first time, young Tom found himself all alone. He felt an intoxicating sense of freedom. At last, nobody could tell him what to do. At the same time, though, he had nobody to rely on. Nobody, that is, except himself.

Tom did have a job, though, as a messenger for Western Union. As he rode the Fifth Avenue bus on his way to deliver packages, he would look out the window and wonder at all the differences he saw along the way. Downtown, the buildings were beautiful, clean, and well maintained. But Uptown, there were rundown buildings with laundry hanging on strings across narrow alleys. Why do some people have so little, he wondered, while others have so much? And how could people who have so little move up in life?

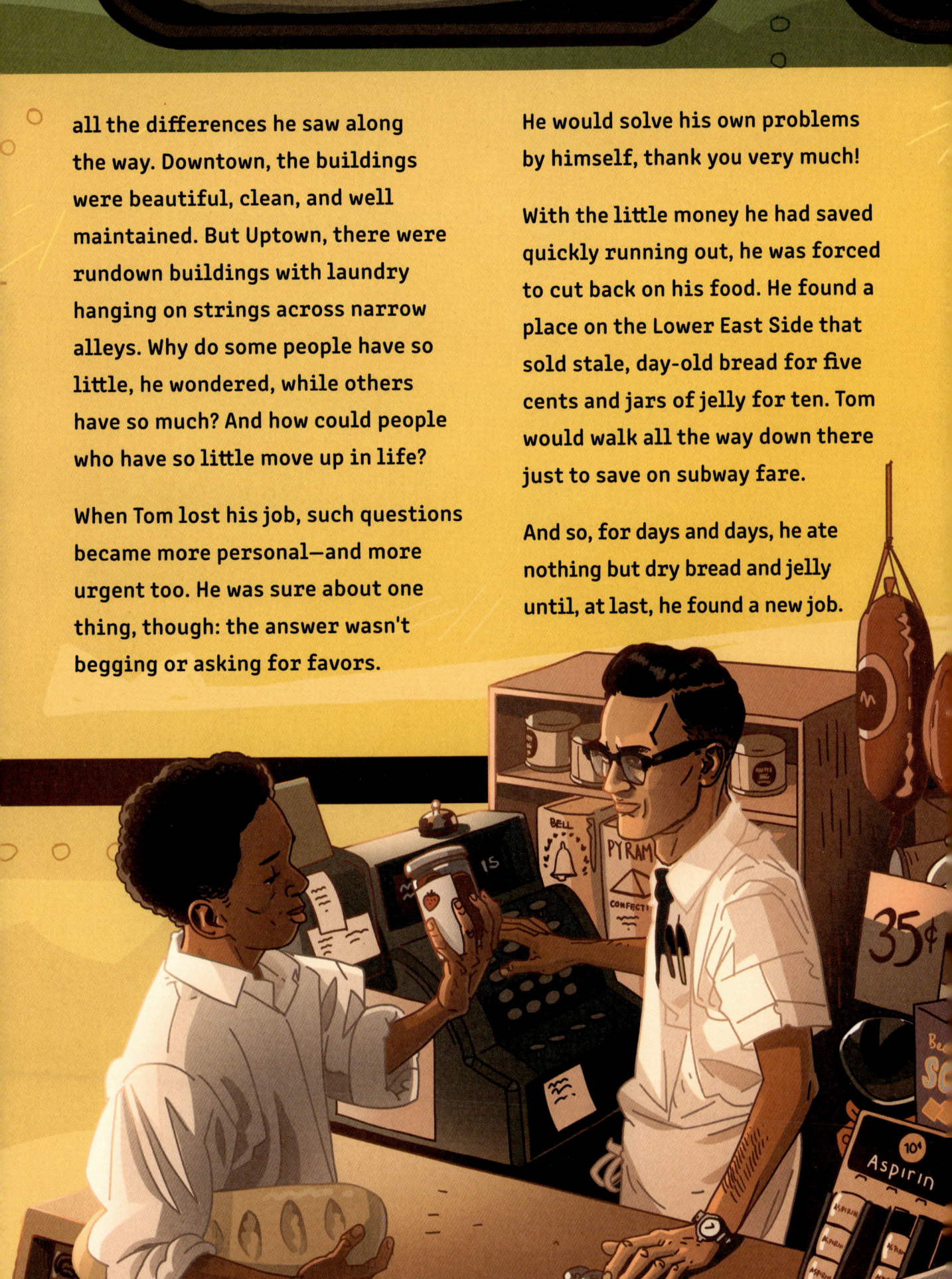

When Tom lost his job, such questions became more personal—and more urgent too. He was sure about one thing, though: the answer wasn't begging or asking for favors.

He would solve his own problems by himself, thank you very much!

With the little money he had saved quickly running out, he was forced to cut back on his food. He found a place on the Lower East Side that sold stale, day-old bread for five cents and jars of jelly for ten. Tom would walk all the way down there just to save on subway fare.

And so, for days and days, he ate nothing but dry bread and jelly until, at last, he found a new job.

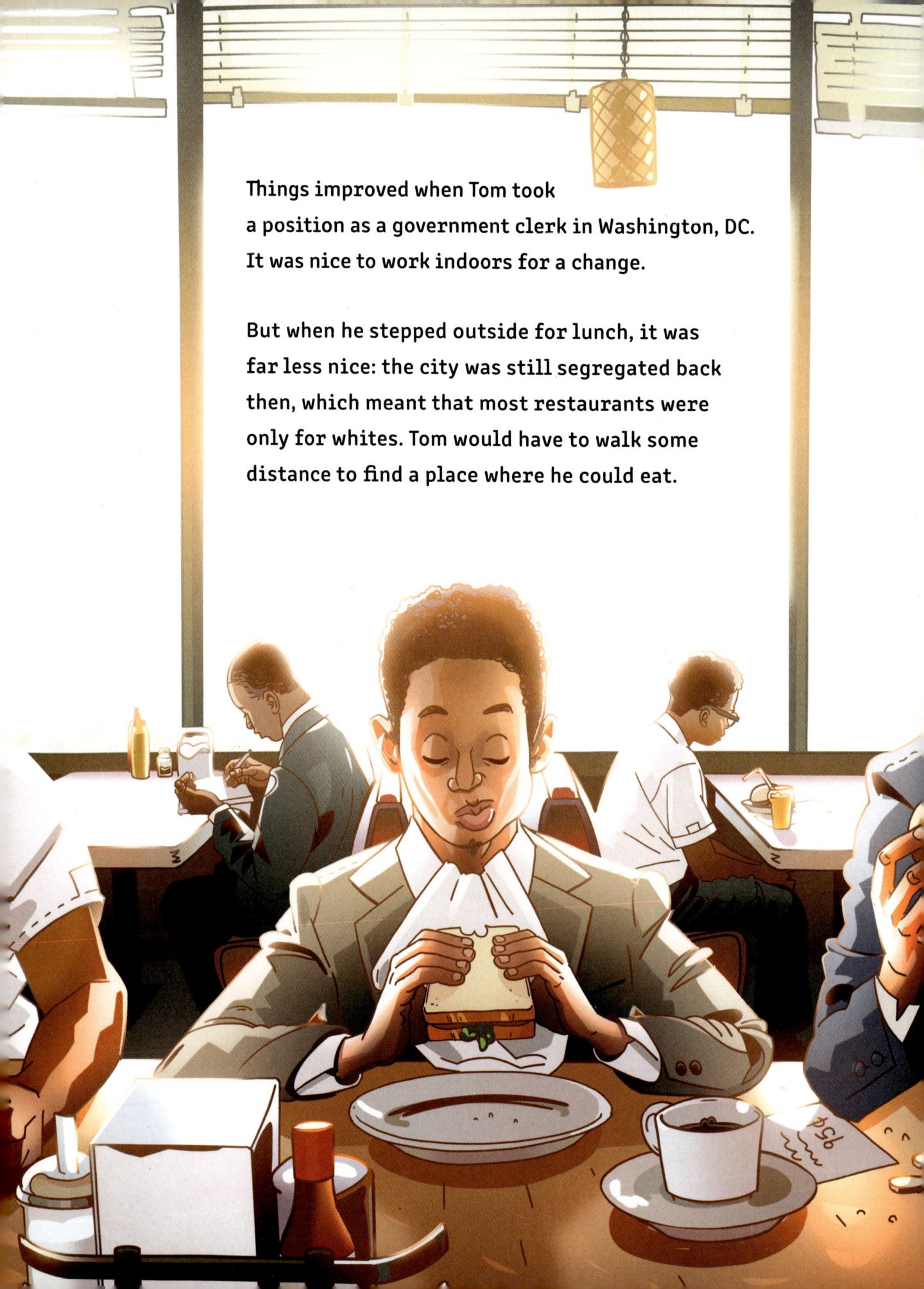

Things improved when Tom took a position as a government clerk in Washington, DC. It was nice to work indoors for a change.

But when he stepped outside for lunch, it was far less nice: the city was still segregated back then, which meant that most restaurants were only for whites. Tom would have to walk some distance to find a place where he could eat.

There was still another problem with this job: it bored him.

Tom began to feel that he had made a serious mistake. He realized he should have never left school.

But he wasn't the kind of guy to sit around feeling sorry for himself. He didn't dwell on the past or blame Aunt Molly, their poverty, his teachers, or American society.

Instead, he turned his attention to the future and took matters into his own hands. He decided to enroll in night classes.

Now, instead of going home to relax after work, he spent his evenings catching up on his education.

This time, Tom took his education seriously. Eventually he moved from night classes to a full-time degree—first at Howard University, and then at Harvard, Columbia, and the University of Chicago. Once done with his studies, he became a professor at Cornell University.

The man who had grown up in a home with no electricity or running hot water had become Professor Thomas Sowell!

And now, as an esteemed professor, Thomas was in a position to help others. And he was about to learn a valuable lesson about what really helps and what does not.

It all started with a student in one of his classes who seemed like she was in trouble. She came from a faraway country in Africa and her English wasn't so great.

She was also very shy. She was afraid to speak up in class and to ask for help when there was something she didn't understand.

From one week to the next, she fell further and further behind. She sat paralyzed in her chair, hoping Professor Sowell wouldn't ask her to speak.

And then one day he finally did. The class fell silent. All eyes were on her.

"Well?" Professor Sowell said. "What do you think?" But she had no answer. "I don't know," she said, and looked down at her shoes. Her voice was barely more audible than a whisper. Thomas asked her to come see him after class.

Once in his office, she started to cry. Tears ran down her cheeks and fell silently onto her lap. Her family had worked so hard to send her all the way to America, she said. How could she disappoint them by failing out of school?

Her story touched Thomas. He really wanted to help her. Maybe, he thought, he should just give her a passing grade?

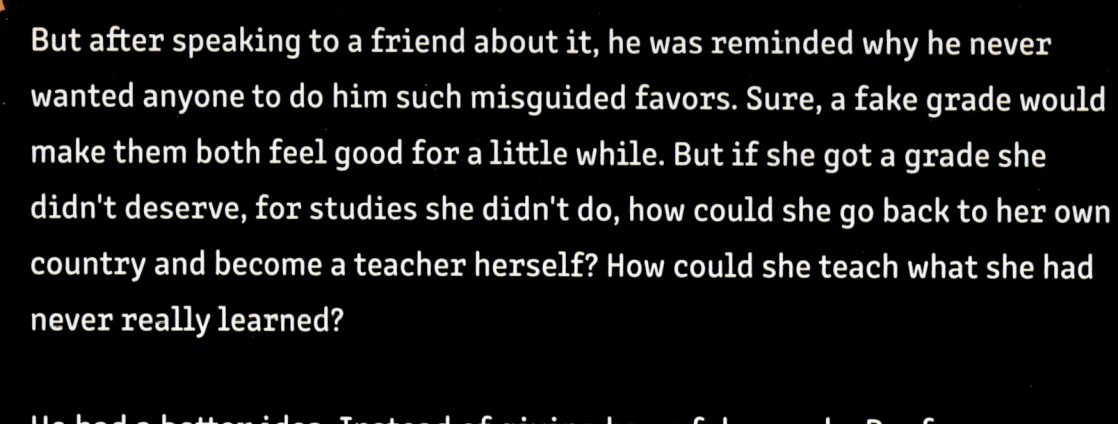

But after speaking to a friend about it, he was reminded why he never wanted anyone to do him such misguided favors. Sure, a fake grade would make them both feel good for a little while. But if she got a grade she didn't deserve, for studies she didn't do, how could she go back to her own country and become a teacher herself? How could she teach what she had never really learned?

He had a better idea. Instead of giving her a fake grade, Professor Sowell offered to tutor her before every class. It was very hard at first, but he was not giving up on her. And what do you know? Little by little she relaxed, she learned, and she began to catch up with the class.

In the end, she earned that passing grade. It wasn't a very high one, but it was hers—the real fruit of her real efforts. Oh, you should have seen her beaming smile when she learned she had succeeded! Against all odds, she'd done it. And most importantly, she'd done it herself.

Thomas Sowell returned to the question of undeserved favors in his many books, lectures, and newspaper articles. He insisted that in the long run, they just don't help people improve their lives, no matter how good the intention. That's because if you give people something they didn't earn, they wouldn't learn how to earn it themselves.

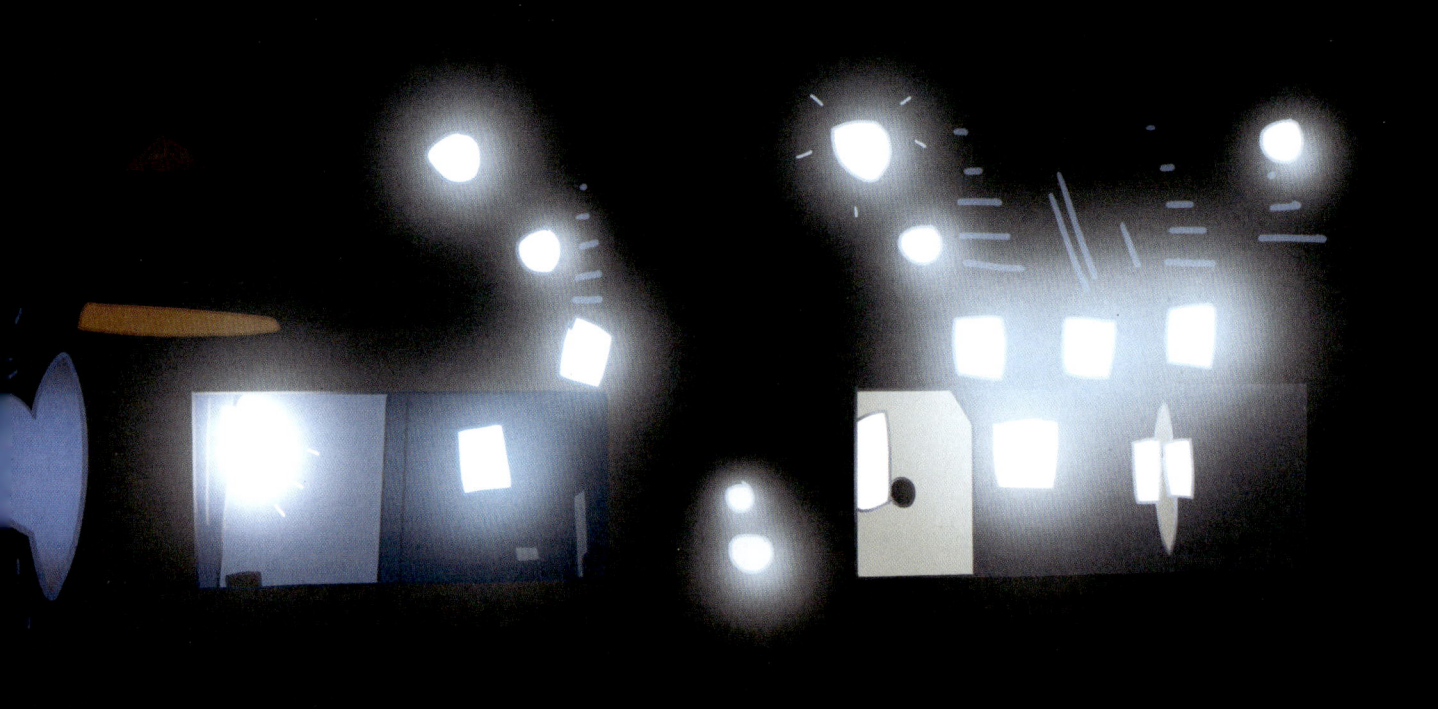

Thomas also practiced what he preached. When he was offered a prestigious job just because he was black, he turned it down. He would not accept a position his accomplishments did not justify. In his eyes, nothing good could come of getting something you didn't really earn.

Thomas Sowell also became famous for speaking out against unequal treatment. He became so famous, in fact, that he was invited to talk to Congress and got into an argument with a senator named Joe Biden—the very same Joe Biden who would later become president of the United States.

Thomas claimed that everyone, regardless of skin color, should receive equal treatment under the law. Unequal treatment was wrong when people's intentions were bad, like with Jim Crow laws in the South. Unequal treatment was also wrong when people's intentions were good, like giving people advantages without regard to their real achievements. That's because, just like fake grades, unearned advantages won't help people succeed in the long run.

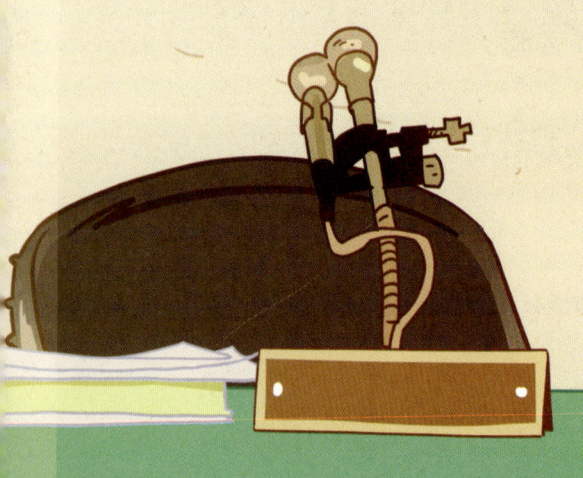

· Mr. THURMOND ·

Some senators—and many had good intentions—did not agree. But as you might have guessed, Thomas didn't mind. He wasn't about to back down, even in the face of very powerful people—just like he hadn't backed down in the face of bigger, taller boys on the baseball field. He didn't care if his opinions were unpopular. What mattered to him was standing up for what he thought was right.

Some powerful people did appreciate Thomas Sowell's opinions. One of them was President Ronald Reagan. The president wanted Thomas to serve in his cabinet as secretary of labor. Thomas said he was honored but he would have to turn the offer down. Later, he was offered the post of secretary of education too. But again, he turned it down. That's because he believed he could do more good by writing books.

And time has proven him right. His ideas have taken on a life of their own.

Thomas Sowell's words continue to influence the hearts and minds of all sorts of people. You can find his wisdom everywhere: on social media, in classrooms, in newspapers, in podcasts and videos, and on bookshelves around the world. You, too, have just encountered them, right here in this very book you're holding in your hand.

And as surely as the sun rises, you will find yourself one day—maybe tomorrow, maybe even years from now—thinking about the ideas of Thomas Sowell.

And maybe one day, if you find yourself in a tough spot of your own, these ideas will help you find a way to make things better.

7 INTERESTING FACTS ABOUT
Thomas Sowell

THOMAS SOWELL WAS A PHOTOGRAPHER IN THE UNITED STATES MARINE CORPS.

HIS SON, JOHN, WAS ALMOST 4 YEARS OLD WHEN HE BEGAN TO SPEAK. JOHN TURNED OUT TO BE EXCEPTIONALLY BRIGHT. AS A YOUTH, HE WAS A CHESS CHAMPION.

THOMAS SOWELL HAS WRITTEN MORE THAN 30 BOOKS. ONE OF THEM WAS ABOUT LATE-TALKING CHILDREN.

?

HE'S KNOWN FOR HIS WITTY OBSERVATIONS. HE ONCE SAID: "IT'S AMAZING HOW MUCH PANIC ONE HONEST MAN CAN SPREAD AMONG A MULTITUDE OF HYPOCRITES."

$

HE BEGAN TO BELIEVE IN THE VIRTUES OF THE FREE MARKET AFTER HE WORKED AS AN ECONOMIST FOR THE UNITED STATES GOVERNMENT.

ONE OF HIS TEACHERS AT THE UNIVERSITY OF CHICAGO WAS MILTON FRIEDMAN, WHO WON THE NOBEL PRIZE IN ECONOMICS. FRIEDMAN WAS ONE OF THE MOST FAMOUS ADVOCATES OF FREE-MARKET CAPITALISM.

HE KEPT WRITING WEEKLY SYNDICATED COLUMNS UNTIL HE WAS 86 YEARS OLD. HE STOPPED SO HE COULD FOCUS ON PHOTOGRAPHY.